The Right Support System

Archbishop

Q.S. Caldwell, Th.D., D.D.

ROYSTON
Publishing

BK Royston Publishing
P. 0. Box 4321
Jeffersonville, IN 47131
502-802-5385
http://www.bkroystonpublishing.com
bkroystonpublishing@gmail.com

Cover Design: LaNorris Blutcher

ISBN-13: 978-1-955063-56-2

Printed in the United States of America

DEDICATION

This Book is dedicated to the following two individuals who are a very important part of my life and ministry.

Dr. Charles B. Gillespie

A Man of faith and a Man of strong will.

Mother Mattie Mansfield a.k.a. "Mother Good"

A most beloved Woman of God whose influence shaped my ministry and foundational upbringing.

A WORD FROM THE AUTHOR

"You can do anything as long as you have the passion, the drive, the focus, and the support."

--Sabrina Bryan

Support is something that is needed in ever field of human endeavor. We need one another to survive and develop because it is impossible to do anything alone. No man or woman achieves great exploits without having the right people reinforce their personhood in accountability while undergirding their efforts.

Seasons of life, particularly in development and trial, sort out those who are assigned to us versus those who are simply associated with us. If you look back, you may see that at different points in your life, you depend on different people for different things. Contingent upon our age, needs, wants and desires, we have turned to different people in our support system to help with different areas of our lives. As we grow and age, some of us feel that have confidence in others is a flaw or limitation that is not true! Having the right support system is not an indication of weakness, but it is a mark of strength.

Equally, it is just as important to be a support to others, as it is to be supported. Having the right support system is a two-way street, we need to support those in our lives just as those people support us. When it comes to having support that fits, you will need trusted pastors, leaders, colleagues, friends, family, and peers you can be sure of when times get tough. Ideally, you will have created these covenant bonds throughout the various periods of your life that have proven their unwavering presence.

The truth is that the right support systems can help you in every facet of life! Your support system can play an essential role in your holistic growth. The right support system can help you find new opportunities and connect with influential people that fuel your future forward. I pray that as you read this book you will discover what it means to be the "right support" as well as be supported by the "right support system."

In Christ I Abide,

Archbishop Q.S. Caldwell, Th.D., D.D.
Primate
Celebration of Praise Ministries, Inc.

THE SEAL OF THE CHIEF APOSTLE · CELEBRATION OF PRAISE MINISTRIES, INC.

Table of Contents

FOREWORD

The right support system is very essential for success whether in the marketplace or ministry. When dealing with leadership as part of the support system, there are two components that the support system experience.

The first one is training and development and the second one is you are in a position of authority. Therefore, you have great responsibilities. You must operate in the position of offense (being proactive) and defense (being protective).

In this book, Archbishop Q.S. Caldwell, deals with the principles of having the right support system in place. His writings exemplify the perpetual strength, stability, and security of this system.

I would not only suggest but advise

both the marketplace and ministry to invest in your support system and even yourself by ordering this phenomenal book.

Atavia Barnes, CEO
ASB Consulting Firm
Four Times Author

FOREWORD

While I have not known Dr. Caldwell for a long time, in the short time I have known him, he always highlights the distinct difference in meaning between "Chronos" and "Kairos" time.

While Chronos time is linear and repetitive with its own advantages, Kronos time is "event specific, epochal and impactful." So, my meeting and acquaintance with Dr. Caldwell was more infused with Kairos time than mere Chronos time. It is on this basis that I take pen in hand to write a brief review of his book titled, "The Right Support System."

Any book that seeks to lay out principles and pathways for Christian living, especially for those in Ministry, must first be substantiated by the life of the author.

My meeting with Dr. Caldwell and my subsequent acquaintance with him, deeply impressed me with the genuineness of his life, passion for service, his pioneering spirit, missionary zeal and his commitment to follow his Lord and Master, Jesus Christ! These attributes lived out, provide the necessary motive and impetus for anyone to read and imbibe what Dr. Caldwell has to share from the rich repertoire of his life and ministry.

The present brokenness and fractured nature of individuals, our society, governance and the world, with no coherent solutions on the horizon, highlights the message of Scripture, that only the ultimate coming of the Lord to set His creation right, can be the "Hope" on which we depend. The work that began with the Resurrection morning, impels us and the Church to realize the reality of that Hope and hence commit ourselves to the call of our Lord to, "Go and make disciples of all nations..."

It is in commitment to and deep belief in that Hope, that I believe Dr. Caldwell has written to encourage those of us who aspire to follow in our Master's footsteps, to look at "The Right Support System" as a critical enabler of achieving what the Lord commanded us to do – that is to "Go into all the world and make disciples."

In explaining what he understands as the "Right Support System," Dr. Caldwell would have us look at three components of a "Right Support system" – Position vs Assignment; Right Fit vs. Forced Fit and Regrouping for the Sake of Recovery.

In discussing Position vs. Assignment, the author looks at the critical difference between the two and concludes that what we were made for was the "Assignment" God has for us and "Position" is only an enabler to accomplish our Assignment. Reversing that would be catastrophic! He then rightly concludes that, "The assignment is not for the position, but the position is for the assignment." Dr. Caldwell provides us a rich understanding of "Assignment," when he writes, "Each of us are to be used as vessels in other people's lives for the sacred aim of giving hope, sustaining life, recovering the lost and reviving those who need spiritual resuscitation. The position and assignment, given by God, calls us all to a communal accountability and responsibility."

In his exposition of understanding the necessity of the "Right Fit vs. Forced Fit," Dr. Caldwell highlights the necessity of finding the right people who "fit" and thus help you achieve your God given assignment. "Relational Chemistry" is important in finding and keeping those who provide the "right fit." He points out what happens when you have the "wrong fit" and how that can be a detriment to achieving the Assignment God has given you. Pointers to those who can provide the right fit are described by the author as follows. "Personality, Lifestyle, Spirituality and Intellectual capacity are all categories to consider in establishing the "right fit" and determining if an individual can support you adequately in pursuit of your purpose."

Dr. Caldwell points out the "Essential Nature of Support." After carefully defining what "Support" means as encompassing, "Presence, Participation and Push," he points out its essential nature when he states, "When we have the right support system, we develop an unwavering sense of trust in those who walk alongside of us in our position and in our assignment because they ensure that we will not fall."

In the Chapter discussing "Regrouping," the author discusses the important issue of when we face setbacks and failings in completing our Assignment. God's matchless grace to get us back on track forms the bedrock for this discussion. He then provides us the idea of how "balance" and "boundaries" help us in ensuring we do not revert to failures and setbacks. He states, "Life is meant to be enjoyed, but it is to be enjoyed in the will of God." In this one statement is encapsulated the richness of God's Word as "a lamp unto our feet and a light unto our path" (Psalm 119:105).

Dr. Caldwell's book is filled with rich aphorisms too numerous to highlight, but would be useful for anyone looking to learn from a seasoned practitioner of the faith. His points are made with references to Scripture and Biblical characters like Jacob and David that provide apt color to the points being made. The author maintains the appropriate Biblical balance between Gods Sovereign will, His abounding grace and man's moral culpability for which he is held accountable by a righteous God. Dr. Caldwell's insights and prescriptions provided in his book will serve any Christian and especially those in Ministry and Leadership, a treasure trove of guidance that will help us prove effective in the calling to which God has called us.

Rajan S. Mathews

President – Nyack College, Seminary, Graduate Schools

Chapter 1

The Position vs.
The Assignment

Assignment
noun
as·sign·ment | \ ə-ˈsīn-mənt

a: The act of assigning something the assignment of a task.
b: A position, post, or office to which one is assigned.

Position
noun
po·si·tion | \ pə-ˈzi-shən

a: Relative place, situation, or standing.
b: To put in a certain position.

Chapter 1
Position vs. The Assignment

Psalm 75:7 (KJV)

But God is the judge: he putteth down one, and setteth up another.

Ephesians 2:10 (KJV) *declares, "For we are His workmanship, created in Christ Jesus to good works, which God has before ordained that we should walk in them.* Every person that has ever been born, existed or lived in the earth was intended to do so by God. Before God formed each of us, He decided what function that He desired for us to engage in on earth. God placed both a purpose and orchestrated the series of processes in our lives that he would use to develop it into its mature state. He strategically established and brought into line exactly how He wanted you to serve Him, and then God designed and sculpted you for that task. You are "the way you are" because you were crafted specifically for a particular assignment in the earth. There are no mistakes when it comes to God placing an individual here to activate His divine agenda. We must understand that the plan of God is the priority.

When God puts you in a position, it is for the betterment of someone else. When God ordains an assignment for your life to carry out, it is to accomplish His divine agenda according to his sovereign will. Throughout the course of your life, you will be given an extensive scope of assignments that are specific to the purpose to which your life has been assigned. The purpose of your divine assignment is doing what God wants you to do; having what God wants you to have; going where God wants you to go and then becoming who God ultimately wants you to become in this life.

The assignment of God has nothing to do with your preference or desire to do a certain thing. God has given each of us an assignment based on what He has placed on the inside of us. These divine attributes that are found, on the inside of you, are not random or carelessly placed. God is intentional in every investment he makes. God, by the means of investing said purpose in the life of any believer, desires what he placed on the inside of you to come alive and multiply in numerous ways.

God's methodology for preparing us for the assignment and position often seems illogical to us, especially when it comes to trying to reason with our humanity.

Isaiah 55:8-9 (KJV) says, *"For my thoughts are not your thoughts, neither are your ways my ways, saith the LORD. For as the heavens are higher than the earth, so are my ways higher than your ways, and my thoughts than your thoughts."*

God is not confined to our perceptions of what He should do. Often, God does the opposite of what we expect. Our sight, outlook, vision and plans for our lives can be short-sighted. When it comes to both position and assignment, we can be limited by our inability to see what lies ahead and the demands that will be required of us in the future.

There is a sacred responsibility and critical, yet time-sensitive demand on what God has purposed for us to do. Many people wrestle with the tension regarding their assignment from God. Additionally, we often underestimate ourselves because we do not fully understand the purpose to which we exist along with the God's reasoning. Perhaps you are asking God, "Why?" Why did God give me this assignment? Why am I in this specific place or current location? What is the purpose in me being connected to this group of people? Why is my life this way? Why was my childhood filled with trauma? Why did I have to endure adversity and systematic difficulties? Why did I have to endure this type of pain? God has given each of us a direct assignment that cannot be avoided. Will it require preparation? Yes!

Will it require discipline while developing character in difficult situations, uncomfortable positions and journeying into unfamiliar places? Yes! Does it feel unreachable or bigger than us in certain moments? Yes. Does the big picture perspective seem blurry without all of the details? Absolutely, it does. However, there is a grace that is given for its completion. God will never send you out with a mandate to perform a task and set you up for failure. What we must come to resolve is this: The assignment is not for the position, but the position is for the assignment. At times, the position we may find ourselves in might not entail the most pleasant of circumstances. Even in the hostile and awkward positions we find ourselves in at various times along the way, we are being qualified to carry out our ultimate assignment through experience and preparation.

Jacob's Conflict: Wrestling with Purpose to Discover "The Why"

The narrative that chronicles Jacob's struggle with God teaches us resilience in the pursuit of God amid uncomfortable situations that cause anguish and agony.

Genesis 32:24-32 (KJV) - *And Jacob was left alone; and there wrestled a man with him until the breaking of the day.*

And when he saw that he prevailed not against him, he touched the hollow of his thigh; and the hollow of Jacob's thigh was out of joint, as he wrestled with him.

And he said, Let me go, for the day breaketh. And he said, I will not let thee go, except thou bless me.

And he said unto him, What is thy name? And he said, Jacob.
And he said, Thy name shall be called no more Jacob, but Israel: for as a prince hast thou power with God and with men, and hast prevailed.

Jacob is a bible character who depicts the power and grace of God to change, renew and find purpose. He is presented in the biblical text for his crafty and fraudulent behavior. These attributes emerge at the forefront of his narrative, particularly when it comes to his twin brother Esau. However, after being conquered by God in a wrestling match, Jacob received God's blessings. God gives him a new name – Israel. Jacob teaches us that the road to both position and assignment can be unconventional. Jacob's path to the transformational encounter with God and discovering his "why" began when he returned home to Canaan with his family. Jacob had served his father-in-law Laban. Subsequently, Jacob receives urgent news that Esau is coming to take his life because of his previous deceptions. Jacob finds himself afraid for both his life and his family's as well. Fearful and afraid, he packs them up and sends them ahead of himself to prevent them from seeing any harm. As a result, he is left by himself. While there, he enters into a wrestling match with God until the breaking of the next day.

Jacob was not just in conflict with his "inner self," but he found himself in direct opposition to God. Jacob was lost and negligent of his position as patriarch and his assignment to become a part of the lineage of Christ. God desired relationship with Jacob, as he does so many of us, in order to reveal what needs to be seen. Jacob had to rid himself of his feebleness of self-sufficiency, dishonesty, and deception. One touch, on the socket of his hip, pushed Jacob to a place of submission and caused him to truthfully acknowledge his complete necessity for God.

Jacob received a new name– Israel as indicated in Genesis 32:28. This name was accompanied with a new identity. The new name he received detached him from his troubled past and gave him a fresh start.

Moving forward, he was able to embrace his position in becoming a person with a divine assignment to establish the Israelite nation.

Jacob's story teaches us that your will has to be stronger than your struggle. When a person holds onto their hurt internally, they restrict their ability to function. These restrictions effect their emotional, psychological, and physical states. In turn, they punish themselves and paralyze their assignment because they have not appropriately processed their pain. There has to come a time when we decide to separate from the place of our pain. Jacob experienced being isolated from people.

In that same way, God will shrink your circle in order to save your life. Subsequently, we must also separate the process from the assignment.

This is why Jacob was able to live past the struggle and still be successful. He did not allow the pain to become problematic in his pursuit of total change. Instead, he persevered beyond the intensity of his present moment and contended for an unknown future that was in the hands of a known God. God honored his ability to pursue Him at all cost and without reservation. Jacob was not desperate, but rather demonstrated a level of determination that was needed to achieve a desired result. In that same manner, we must learn to remain consistent and committed in not letting go or losing our focus on what we need or desire.

David's Purpose, Position and Assignment:
From the Pasture to the Palace

David is a prime example of being positioned for the assignment. David, the 7th son of Jesse, begins his preparation tending sheep of his father on the backside of the mountain.

1 Samuel 16:11-13 (KJV) –

"And Samuel said unto Jesse, Are here all thy children? And he said, there remaineth yet the youngest, and, behold, he keepeth the sheep.

And Samuel said unto Jesse, Send and fetch him: for we will not sit down till he come hither. And he sent, and brought him in. Now he was ruddy, and withal of a beautiful countenance, and goodly to look to.

And the Lord said, Arise, anoint him: for this is he. Then Samuel took the horn of oil and anointed him in the midst of his brethren: and the Spirit of the Lord came upon David from that day forward. So, Samuel rose up, and went to Ramah."

David was called for his assignment while working in the preparatory phase of his occupation. He was a shepherd in this moment. All of Jesse's sons were presented to the prophet Samuel. However, the oil did not pour. Plainly stated, all of them were called but David was chosen. In that same right, Matthew 22:14 says, *"For many are called, but few are chosen."* He would go on to be anointed again 3 different times to be exact. However, tending the sheep that belong to his father was a precursor to leading a people as King. David was a man anointed and purposed by God to accomplish a specific task. He would become the 'Man After God's Own Heart and one of the greatest Kings of Israel!' David was called for a purpose and chosen for an assignment.

In 1 Samuel 16:1-23, we discover this portion of Samuel, specifically Chapters 16-31, emphasizes "The Rise of David." From now on, David is the center of the biblical story and Saul is seen chiefly as the number one enemy of David. In Chapter 16, Samuel anoints David as the next king and God has finally chosen His man to rule over Israel. Although God did select Saul, He selected him to please the selfish demands of the Israelites for a king so that they could be like the other nations. The Bible reveals that God had plans for Israel to have a king at some point. This is found in Deuteronomy 17:14-20. Saul was not in God's perfect timing. Nevertheless, He gave Israel a king after their own desire – one whom the text says was "from his shoulders and upward was higher than any of the people." 1 Samuel 9:2 says, *"And he had a son, whose name was Saul, a choice young man, and handsome: and there was not among the children of Israel a more handsome person than he: from his shoulders and upward he was higher than any of the people."* Saul was a "man's man" and had the image of the king desired by Israel.

However, David was God's man. Though he was handsome in the flesh, the scripture describes him as "of a beautiful countenance." He did not have the imposing physical appearance that brought awe. He was rather young and "ruddy." However, the Lord chose and purposed David to accomplish his agenda and his work. David was called out, called to, and positioned for an assignment. David was called out of the pasture, called to the house, and anointed to be positioned as King with an assignment to lead the God's chosen people. Samuel, a priest and oracle of God, clearly delivers the message of the almighty to Saul informing him of the end of his reign and thus solidifying the affirmation of David as the future king. 1 Samuel 13:14 *says, "But now thy kingdom shall not continue: the LORD hath sought him a man after his own heart, and the LORD hath commanded*

him to be captain over his people,
because thou hast not kept that which
the LORD commanded thee."

David, therefore, became "the man who was raised up on high, the anointed of the God of Jacob, and the sweet psalmist of Israel. He went forth to fulfill all God's will and served his own generation by the will of God. There is an undeniable difference that we see between Saul and David. One of them impressed men by his exterior appearance; the other impressed God by the condition of his heart.

However, David would encounter tremendous adversity and struggle on his way to the throne. He learned so many lessons in perseverance, defending the fold, developing, nurturing, guiding, and safeguarding. All of these experiences would give him the needed skillsets to take into a more refined space as King of Israel. These skills would not only have to be honed, but David's humanity and persona would have to undergo necessary processing to build him into the leader that God required him to be for his people. Being a king was the position, but his assignment was to rule under the providence of God and obey the law as God commanded. In other words, he was a man in authority but under authority. Not only consider the life of David, yet there is a premier example of not just positioning, but the acceptance of an assignment in Jesus the Christ. Jesus was the Son of God, but he was also the Savior of the world.

Jesus' Embrace of Purpose: Taking Position with the Acceptance of His Divine Assignment

Luke 22:41-43 (KJV) - *And he was withdrawn from them about a stone's cast, and kneeled down, and prayed, Saying, Father, if thou be willing, remove this cup from me: nevertheless not my will, but thine, be done. And there appeared an angel unto him from heaven, strengthening him.* Jesus submitted his will to embrace the Will of the Father in The Garden of Gethsemane. His humanity wanted to say no, but his divinity said yes! Jesus finds himself in a defining moment. Jesus yielded to the Will of the Father knowing the cost of his consent to this assignment.

People, from all walks of life, struggle with yielding because we lack the ability of trusting God's decision despite our own places of doubt. Too often, there is an internal conflict within regarding God's divine decision. We have the innate tendency to disagree concerning each of our life's direction, purpose and assignment based on carnal justifications. When we stop trying to reason in our minds, we would become more apt to operate in immediate obedience. As a result, our trust in the Lord would increase. We must take comfort in knowing that God would never do anything outside of our best interest. We fail to recognize that God has seen the outcome before we face the obstacle. If He is aware of the obstacle surrounding the present situation concerning our position and assignment, he will give us both the grace and strength to endure the processes that prepare us to undertake it. The evidence of God's hand is the ability to endure beyond the place of your limitation.

Jesus had the ability to stop the process of his own crucifixion. However, it was the power of choice that eliminated Satan's strategy of condemnation and executed God's plan for redemption of the entire human race. Jesus' actions encourage us to follow through and finish even when it feels as if we are by ourselves. As a believer, with both a position and assignment within the kingdom, you must recognize that God is sovereign. Just because God is silent, does not mean he is sightless. God is aware, concerned, and attentive to the posture of your heart and where you are currently placed. God does not disregard your humanity, but he empowers your spirit man while in the process through the power of the Holy Ghost. The Holy Ghost converts our perspective. What you would normally view as a problem, is a place where you can recognize His undeniable presence, see the solution at hand, and receive his promise.

Jesus teaches us that our yes to God becomes a place of access. When we say yes to the Lord, it opens up the opportunity for God to act. Our yes to the position and assignment of God, for our lives, is the exit that becomes the entrance to our purpose. Our innate human resistance shows the fragility of our humanity while humility shows the willingness of one to be malleable. Jesus resolves that he is called for a purpose and chosen for an assignment. God positions us for the assignment. We must make the choice to align with the agenda of God. Positioning comes by way of groundwork, training, and vetting for purposes that are of sacred use. Every task that we undertake is sacred. We must accept the fact that the position comes with "weighty" responsibilities. These responsibilities must be stewarded and never neglected. There is a demand for accuracy, awareness, and oversight in managing what we have been positioned to oversee. From jobs to family-life, we must fully avail ourselves to the commitment of sacred responsibility.

The word of God in Colossians 3:23 (KJV) – *"And whatsoever ye do, do it heartily, as to the Lord, and not unto men."* The assignment sets the course for the process that we must undergo. It is our means of development that both groom and grow us for the assignment that lies ahead for each of us. The method is never easy. In fact, it can carry excruciating discomfort and pain. However, it produces in us a measure of discipline and determination which become the catalyst for our future successes. The position is the place or posture that God holds us in for the duration of the assignment.

As the Son of God, he was tasked with the assignment of redeeming and reconciling humanity back to the God, the Father. Jesus teaches us through his intentional demonstration that, "The heart only sees the present, but the will of God sees the future."

Matthew 27:45-47 (KJV) - *"Now from the sixth hour there was darkness over all the land unto the ninth hour. And about the ninth hour Jesus cried with a loud voice, saying, Eli, Eli, lama sabachthani? That is to say, My God, my God, why hast thou forsaken me? Some of them that stood there, when they heard that, said, This man calleth for Elias."*

God supported Jesus in silence to show us that presence is more important words. God promises in the latter part of Hebrews 13:5 (KJV) *"……….. God himself has said, "I will never leave you; never will I forsake you."* Words are affirming, but they do not necessarily constitute action. Words are a carrier of will and intent. Words expose the heart of men. Presence reveals the hand of God. Psalm 46:1 (KJV) - *God is our refuge and strength, a very present help in trouble.*

We cannot live in disappointment because we are never without the presence of the Lord. We must not allow our misplaced expectations concerning the position within the assignment to lead us into a posture of faithlessness.

With God, we are never out of options, outcomes or opportunities. The ability of God is not confined to our inability to navigate a problem. The ability of God is linked to the push that is needed for us to seek and secure a solution. As believers, we must internalize that the fullness of God's support is not predicated on if he does things our way. His plan reveals his commitment to the outcome of your life. Jeremiah 1:12 (KJV) - *Then said the Lord unto me, "Thou hast well seen, for I will hasten My word to perform it."*

Jesus was sent into the world, by God, to preserve the life of others. When we understand the intent of positioning and assignment, we can accept that each of us are the object of God's life-preserving work of fulfillment regarding the Kingdom agenda here on earth. It is God, not us, who puts all of us where we are supposed to be. Each of us are to be used as vessels in other people's lives for the sacred aim of giving renewed hope, sustaining life, recovering the lost, and reviving those who need spiritual resuscitation. The position and assignment, given by God, calls us all to a communal accountability and responsibility.

We must unapologetically go and do those things that preserve the lives of people around us!

Unearthing our assignment and discerning the path that God would desire for us to take is key. We can only accurately discern through seeking God and petitioning for Him to reveal to us all that we need to know not just about the assignment, but ourselves as well. Self-awareness is key, and it comes by way of intricate, yet intimate self-reflection. Ask yourself, "What has God spoken to you about where you are and what He has called you to do?" Fulfilling the assignment of God requires that you focus on the explicit directives, neglect distractions and execute from a place of radical obedience. God requires completion of the assignment he has entrusted to you.

Chapter 2

Right Fit vs. Forced Fit:

The Necessity of Relational Chemistry

The Seal of the Chief Apostle
Celebration of Praise Ministries Inc.

Chapter 2

Right Fit vs. Forced Fit:
The Necessity of Relational Chemistry

In 2 Samuel, Chapter 6, David returns the Ark of the Covenant to Jerusalem. David summons the elite of his men to bring the Ark to Jerusalem. The return of the Ark of the Covenant was critically important to establishing a place of worship that was centralized for the entire nation of Israel. The Ark was not just an ordinary box. First, the significance of this vessel was rooted in the fact that God have Moses an explicit directive 400 years before David's existence, to undertake the task of building a "box" or "chest" that would be the representation of his presence and power. Second, it was solid gold and was complete by a lid coupled with ornamentation called the "Mercy Seat."

"The Ark of God was 3 feet 9 inches (1.15 meters) long, 2 feet 3 inches (.68 meter) wide and 2 feet 3 inches (.68 meter) high. In it were the tablets of the law that Moses brought down from Mount Sinai, a jar of manna, and Aaron's rod that miraculously budded as a confirmation of his leadership. The ark of God represented the immediate presence and glory of God in Israel." (Davis, 1985)

David had a high priority assignment. This was a tremendous undertaking that required obedience, attention to detail, and extreme reverence. David considered it a great task to bring the Ark back to its rightful place in Israel. No longer would the Ark be in a place of obscurity in foreign lands, but it would be brought back to the place of prominence and promise. The Ark represented the presence and glory of God. It is important to note that the only mention of the Arks return was when it came back from the land of the Philistines in 1 Samuel 7:1. It sat at the house of Abinadab for 20 years. David sought, with sincere intent, to bring back to the consciousness of the people the meaning of the presence and glory of God in Israel.

In 2 Samuel 6:1-2, David and gathers together the chosen men of Israel. This number consisted of 30,000 men and they went up from Baale of Judah to bring the Ark of God up from that place.

Verse 14-20 says, *"And David danced before the Lord with all his might; and David was girded with a linen ephod. So David and all the house of Israel brought up the ark of the Lord with shouting, and with the sound of the trumpet. And as the ark of the Lord came into the city of David, Michal Saul's daughter looked through a window, and saw king David leaping and dancing before the Lord; and she despised him in her heart. Then David returned to bless his household. And Michal the daughter of Saul came out to*

*meet David, and said, How
glorious was the king of Israel to
day, who uncovered himself to
day in the eyes of the handmaids
of his servants, as one of the vain
fellows shamelessly uncovereth
himself!*

David did not hold anything back in his own expression of worship. He did not dance out of obligation, but out of heartfelt worship. He was glad to bring the Ark of the LORD into Jerusalem according to God's word. David's wife Michal did not appreciate David's exuberant worship. She felt it was not dignified for the King of Israel to express his emotions before God. In that same right, people will question your actions when they do not understand your relationship!

David teaches us an important lesson that we must follow the will of God despite being misjudged by the misrepresentations of outsiders.

David and Micah were married. They were connected in the bonds of matrimonial covenant. Nevertheless, David and Micah lacked chemistry. They were joined physically, but not spiritually. Micah was connected to him, but not to his assignment. Micah was not open to totality of who David was. She was familiar with his role as a king, but not as a servant of God.

Puzzles are unique in the fact that each piece has a significant place and function that contributes to the final image on the front of the box. Each piece has a particular shape, size and function. Each piece carries a specific place of importance and would distort the picture if positioned out of place. I learned while putting the pieces of puzzles together, that you cannot force pieces of the puzzle into places where they do not fit. It not only leads to your frustration but can, in turn, hinder the piece by continually being forced into a space that it was not made for in the first place.

Micah was out of synch with David and his assignment. She was not a "right fit." Therefore, she was a hindrance and not a help. This is an issue that can definitely speak to the contemporary context of support in ministry relationships and subsequent chemistry. It takes a special person to connect with a chosen vessel. Chemistry, without question, is the most important thing in working ministry relationships. Chemistry lays the foundation of your desire for a thing. Chemistry is just the beginning of what is to come. When you finally have this type of chemistry with someone, you want to not only keep it, but also to grow it into a full-fledged working relationship that reflects peak productivity.

The goal of consistent chemistry is rooted in starting to develop respect, communication, and trust in your relationship while taking intentional efforts to maintain it. These things come from two people who are not just drawn to each other, but they fit and compliment the individual and their purpose that they are supporting. They have no choice in their mind but to make it work, so that is exactly what they do. People take the time to make it work, rather than throw it away when things get hard, because they know and remember the initial chemistry that created the foundation and the chemistry they still have. They understand that they just cannot live without that. Chemistry is, without question, the key to any working relationship that will obtain success. To recognize relational character, there is one litmus test that is very revealing: Examine the relationships that are already present.

By doing this, you can easily uncover what tomorrow's imprint will be. Personality, Lifestyle, Spirituality, and Intellectual capacity are all categories to consider in establishing the "right fit" and determining if an individual can support you adequately in pursuit of your purpose.

Disposition: This category is inclusive of how well you actually mesh, work together, and get along with another individual in both public and private settings.

Way of Life: People with similar dispositions often have a similar way of life.

Spirituality: Relational chemistry that works, in this particular dynamic, is gauged by how closely your religious or moral standards align.

Intellectual: Does a person possess the capacity to accept your purpose and identify the critical areas they can provide you the necessary support you need to accomplish it?

Knowing who you are and what you are called to do will help you with identifying the people who you have working chemistry with on a regular basis. David's and Micah's narrative shows us a great example on how time reveals conflict in relationships. Discovering how a person reacts in a place of conflict is an important part of understanding the nature of your chemistry with them. Chemistry, in any connection, is the bottom line for the endurance and durability of the working association.

The Essential Nature of Support

Support is defined by the Merriam Webster Dictionary as 1: To endure bravely or quietly: bear. 2: To promote the interests or cause of : To uphold or defend as valid or right : Advocate supports fair play.

In the context of our discussion, support can be summed up as three things I call the 3 P's. Support is Presence, Participation, and Push. Support requires an individual to be present physically, mentally, and emotionally in every situation. Support requires active participation that unselfishly engages a course of action to become involved in the process to pursuing a said goal. Support requires push, which is the needed encouragement and emotional support throughout the course of the endeavor.

Another definition of support is defined as "to keep something or somebody upstanding or in place...to prevent from collapsing."

When we consider the field of architecture, we can all agree that support is essential. Foundations support the weight of the structure. The beams, whether metal or wood, support the roof and the walls. Engineers determine and map out all of the loads a building will need to withstand in order to be fully supported.

Each element relies on the next, within the confines of an interconnected relationship, to comprise what we know as a solid shelter. Without support, whatever we attempt to build, or construct would just fall a part in a major way.

The question that many of us face when examining our current support systems is two-fold. Are we fully supported, and do we have the right support system in place?

The expression of feeling fully supported brings about a sense of steadiness, refuge and security of our well-being. There is a culture of reassurance spiritually, emotionally and psychologically that provides for us a space to be without fear. To be fully supported reassures us that we are secured, and our vulnerabilities are not exposed. We are sincerely covered by people that care to see us become on the other side of the developmental process. When we have the right support system, we develop an unwavering sense of trust in those who walk alongside of us in our position and in our assignment because they ensure that we will not fall.

There are many individuals who are independent and may prefer to go at it alone for the sake of moving faster. Others want to move alone because they view having others alongside them as a distraction. There is no task that we can undertake, in any field, that we can work at by ourselves. The right support system is a vital necessity because a person cannot flourish in isolated spaces. It is essential that people both receive and give support because it is a basic human need that cannot be neglected. With any undertaking, in our personal lives or in ministry, there are so many ups and downs that come with the territory.

Life happens, relationships shift, and things change. We need people who are going to remain constant and provide for us a network of support. "Studies have shown that with a support system, we tend to live longer and healthier lives, and we are able to cope with problems or struggles that arise. Research has also shown that a healthy support network helps us to manage anxiety and depression." (Bledsoe & Setterlund, 2015)

In having the right support system, it creates an opportunity for us to shed loneliness and isolation. Every person desires a person or group of persons they can regularly depend on. We need these people to deal with us in integrity, keep confidentiality, give us constructive feedback coupled with honesty, love all around, and genuinely demonstrate care for our overall well-being with no ulterior motives.

God takes the purpose on your life seriously and will align you with the proper people to aid in the cultivation of that purpose. We must recognize that. As bad as we may want someone supporting our efforts or working with us in a certain area, that particular person or set of persons may not be a right fit for where God is taking you.

Romans 15:2 says, *"We should help others do what is right and build them up in the Lord."* God desires that we connect with people who share our ideals and values. We should steer clear of those who are unsupportive, discouraging, and that fail to push you towards the accomplishment of the divine assignment set before you. The right support system consists of uplifting, positive people, who are not afraid to give you heartfelt and sometimes difficult-to-hear advice. Those types of people are the God-ordained, and the kind we truly need in times of struggle as well as the good, fun, celebratory times in life.

Chapter 3

Regroup for the Sake of Recovery:

Maintaining Essential Balance and Boundaries

The Seal of the Chief Apostle
Celebration of Praise Ministries, Inc.

Chapter 3

Regroup for the Sake of Recovery:

Maintaining Essential Balance and Boundaries

David, even though he was a "Man after God's own Heart," had some severe missteps which created several complicated life situations. These moral failures led to layered sins that affected not just him directly, but those that were attached to him. David sees a woman bathing, from the vantage point of his rooftop, named Bathsheba. David sees this woman and inquires about her. There is no question that David sinned—grievously. David committed adultery, likely coercing Bathsheba along the way, and murdered Uriah. David had to be held accountable for what he did and why he did it. David contested this for quite a while, but eventually God changed the posture of his heart, the course of his actions and ultimately his life.

The prophet Nathan confronts David for his sin and shares what its consequences would be. 2 Samuel 12:16 informs us that God will take extreme measures to ensure we recover all through intentionally walking in the process of sincere repentance that, in turn, leads to complete restoration. The words of the prophet Nathan's prompted David to shift and contemplate his actions. Therefore, David worshipped God. There were consequences of David's sin. As we know, sin always comes with a hefty price tag. David's sin and the consequences he would face would not turn God's love away from David. Even in this narrative, what we come to truly see is the unmatched forgiveness of God. As it is often stated, we cannot out-sin God's mercy and grace. David was a man after God's own heart because he never committed the same sin twice. God honored David because he was honest.

> 2 Samuel 12:11-15 (KJV) - *"This is what the Lord says: I will stir up trouble against you within your own household, and before your own eyes I will take your wives and give them to someone close to you. He will go to bed with your wives in broad daylight. You did this secretly, but I will make this happen in broad daylight in front of all Israel." Then David said to Nathan, "I have sinned against the Lord."*

Nathan replied, "The Lord has taken away your sin; you will not die. But since you have shown total contempt for the Lord by this affair, the son that is born to you must die." Then Nathan went home."

This narrative in the life teaches us an important lesson. Stop trying to hide what God has forgiven you from!

The word regroup is a military term which means to come back together in a tactical formation after dispersal in a retreat. It also means to reorganize for renewed effort after a temporary setback.

When we experience events that shift the trajectory of our lives, there comes a time where we must regroup. We must regroup physically, mentally, emotionally and psychologically. A setback is a testimony to a comeback! Just as David became greater after his struggles, we have an opportunity to emerge better than before.

During the course of the struggle, we find out who we are and what we are made of. We come to understand our strengths and the depths of our weaknesses. We, also, discover the necessity of relationship with God. It is this relationship that fuels not just our progress when things are going well, but our recovery when we acknowledge our inability to restore our own selves.

Oftentimes, in our lives, it is a necessary to regroup after we have undergone a situation which caused us to scatter, use up and disperse our strength. Our strength or vitality fuels our ability to pursue purpose in an effective manner. If our strength is exhausted prematurely, we can find ourselves burned out and unproductive. We must lend the fullness of ourselves to the regimented process of restoration, which is the state of wholeness that comes beyond the place of healing. Healing is the process that precedes wholeness. Wholeness is the state of being complete without lack, deficiency or compromise. This is why taking the time to regroup our mental and physical faculties is essential. Romans 12:2 states, *"And be not conformed to this world: but be ye transformed by the renewing of your mind, that ye may prove what is that good, and acceptable, and perfect, will of God."* A transformed mind enables a person to accept, pursue, and execute the plan of God for their lives unapologetically without reservations.

When life has thrown some unexpected situations our way or we have endured an intense, relentless onslaught we need time to collect ourselves. We not only need the break, but we need the right support system that provides for us a strong social support network. Undergoing conflicts, overcoming obstacles, and living through battles takes a lot out of an individual. There comes a time where a believer, no matter the age or experience, has to push into the presence of God. It is in God's presence that we find strength and hope. God's presence combined with a strong support network allows a person to see the importance of being "tethered or connected."

Although David experienced critical circumstances and crucial calamities, he never found himself outside of the reach of God and those that were near him. God and supportive community were always in the middle of each experience with a posture to receive him again with unconditional love. God was both a compass and counsel. God directed David's decisions and gave instructions regarding strategy to succeed past the places that he had formerly suffered. The same is for each of us!

Maintaining Essential Balance and Boundaries

Boundaries are an essential priority to healthy relationships and, really, a healthy life. Setting and sustaining boundaries is a skill that must be developed.

Boundaries reflect the essence of who you are through your standards, anticipations, moralities, or parameters that you establish to keep yourself feeling safe physically, emotionally, and mentally. Maintaining essential balance reinforced by boundaries is paramount to any person's progress.

Building boundaries goes against our innate human desire to be loved and accepted, so we ignore building them. It is not easy to set and communicate our boundaries, but they are essential ingredients for our health, relationships, and safety. Boundaries give us a sense of power and control over our physical space, thoughts, feelings, and behaviors. What is good to you, is not always good for you. Life is meant to be enjoyed, but to be enjoyed in the will of God.

Leaders and laymen, alike, experience difficulty because they are pulled in so many directions. When we find ourselves overextended, this can lead to a place of compromise. Just because an endeavor carries a "good intent" does not mean that it is "God ordained." Adaptability, within the confines of your assignment is essential. Each day will demand that you execute in a different dynamic. The willingness to embrace change will point the way to engage the slate of tasks that need to be done. The Holy

Spirit speaks to guide you in the place of making effective change. Despite how things may change or fluctuate, staying focused is the priority.

Lastly, you need to be willing to make critical choices. The critical choices are what we call boundaries. If you do not make the hard decisions to establish and reinforce those boundaries, you will never successfully fulfill God's assignment.

The great news is once you make the tough decisions to preserve your peace of mind and protect your best interest, God fills the void left behind with His grace and provision.

His joy and blessing will follow you — when you walk in your Godly assignment. The most fulfilling place for Christian leadership to be is right in the middle of their God given purpose.

CONCLUSION

A Support System is a resource pool that is drawn on selectively to support a person. The support system moves them in a direction of their choice, leaves them stronger, and increases their ability to walk in their assignment free of hindrance. Every support system contains a foundational pool of resources that people can access as they navigate forward. These resources are not just people, but settings and systems of principles. As we move forward into the path that God has designed for each of us, it is helpful to be proactive in making connections to establish covenant and connectivity. The right support system is a group of people who demonstrate competence, care, and commitment to seeing a person become what God desires. Everyone needs a well-developed support system. There are many roles that various people play in providing the needed reinforcement. The other side of the responsibility is of the person to remain committed to establish, maintain and effectively utilize their support system.

The right support systems take effort and energy to preserve. It is important that a person knows that there must be a continual examination of the people who are in our circle of support. This is done to ensure that there is no deadweight holding us back or distractions that pull us further from our assigned place of destiny. We must release those who are detractors from our focus on the task at hand and who will stop at nothing to frustrate efforts to move forward. The right support system consists of people who are reciprocal, equitable and fair. If you are supporting a person in a natural or spiritual endeavor, you must possess the qualities of willingness and availability. As you take your journey forward into the future, there are some things you must remember. The equation for the right support system is simple. The right fit + the right person + At the right time + In the right place = Success

Support Systems include but are not limited to the following:

Role Models – People who can help define goals for positions one might assume in the future. Role models not only show what is possible but also are a source of valuable information about the opportunities and problems associated with a given role.

Common interests – People who share common interests or concerns can be especially important in keeping one motivated, and in sorting out those problems that are primarily those of the individual room problems imposed by the larger system and require collective activity to bring about change in that system.

Close Friends – People who help provide nurturance and caring, who enjoy some of the same interests, and who keep one from becoming isolated and alienated. (Oswald, 2005)

Helpers – People who can be depended upon in a crisis to provide assistance. These people are often experts in solving particular kinds of problems and may not be the type with whom one would choose to have a close personal relationship. (Oswald, 2005)

Respect Competence – People who respect the skills one has already developed and who value the contributions that one makes in a given situation. They are particularly helpful during times of transition when one may be feeling unsure of oneself in developing new skills. (Oswald, 2005)

Referral agent – People who can connect one with resources in the environment through their knowledge of people and organizations. They can refer one to those places where one can obtain needed assistance. (Oswald, 2005)

Challengers – People who can help motivate one to explore new ways of doing things, develop new skills, and work toward the development of latent capabilities. They often are people whom one may not care for as personal friends, but who are demanding of us." (Oswald, 2005)

Having the right support system is central to the experience of all people. Even more, having a community within that support system is paramount. It is community that brings us into a place of belonging. The word community is, without question, central to human experience. Being part of an engaging community gives us a sense of belonging. It enables us to share personal relatedness and support perpetual growth of each other, ourselves and our environment.

A community can be anything from a physical place where geographically people connect, or via a virtual space such as social media groups or private community platforms. Communities bring like-minded people together with similar characteristics and common interests. Every community operates with specific boundaries to meet the needs of that community.

Having a sense of community embraces spirit, character, image and pride and is a vital element of a healthy community. It is a feeling that people within the community matter to one another with a shared faith that their needs will be met through commitment and togetherness. Being a part of a community can make us feel as though we are a part of something greater than ourselves.

The Right Support System will aid us in working through moments of crisis, deal with physical and emotional difficulties, or overload of demands in ministry and life. A good support system can help us cope and return to a safe level of functionality.

The Right people making up the right support systems will bring a level of transformation to your life that will assist in developing new skills, overcome dealing with new situations, and model emotional support that is needed to overcome mental challenges that arise in difficult moments. Support systems, with people who are a "fit," will help an individual reach goals and objectives through a collaborative approach. These pillars of support both function in such a way as to maintain and develop the integrity of any individual in any situation.

REFERENCES

Bibles, N. (2018). *Holy Bible: King James Version*. HARPER USA.

Bledsoe, T. S., & Setterlund, K. A. (2015). Thriving in ministry: Exploring the support systems and self-care practices of experienced pastors. *The journal of family and community ministries, 28*(1), 48-66.

Oswald, R. M. (2005). *How to build a support system for your ministry*. Wipf and Stock Publishers.

Made in the USA
Columbia, SC
06 February 2025

53442704R00065